THE OFFICIAL
wolves
ANNUAL 2009

Written By David Instone

A Grange Publication

© 2008. Published by Grange Communications Ltd., Edinburgh, under licence from Wolverhampton Wanderers Football Club. Printed in the EU.

ISBN 978-1-906211-49-3

Photographs © Action Images.

£6.99

contents...

It wasn't just Wolves' promotion near-miss the previous spring that ensured confidence was high at Molineux as the 2007-08 season kicked off. The club also had a new owner and several new players, three of whom (Michael Gray, Darren Ward and Stephen Elliott) were in the starting line-up for the first game at home to Watford. A fourth, Freddy Eastwood, was on the subs' bench as a decent performance deserved better than a last-gasp 2-1 defeat in front of the teatime live cameras.

Wolves spent again before their next game and Kevin Foley made his debut, along with home-grown youngster Elliott Bennett and on-loan keeper Graham Stack, in the stuttering Carling Cup win against Bradford City, a stunning goal from Jody Craddock adding to Eastwood's opener. Eastwood struck again when the side opened their points account by winning well at Sheffield Wednesday and, after hitting a winning goal for Wales in Bulgaria, the striker returned to Molineux to snatch an unlikely victory from the jaws of defeat with a brace against newly-promoted Blackpool.

Wolves had won three games out of four but the month ended with a reminder that their form was still suspect when they surprisingly crashed out of the Carling Cup at home to a Morecambe side just out of non-League football.

AUGUST

SEPTEMBER

Wayne Hennessy, an increasingly impressive replacement for long-term injury victim Matt Murray, was back in goal for the League trip to Stoke and kept a clean sheet in a hard-fought draw.

After another Eastwood goal for Wales, though, Wolves returned to action after a 14-day break for international matches by losing 3-1 at Bryan Robson's Sheffield United despite Elliott's first goal for them.

The team was in mid-table as they embarked on two successive home matches, only to lose 1-0 to Hull in the first of them. But the follow-up against Norwich four days later was as easy as games come, Foley spectacularly opening his goal account for the club before September ended with a 1-1 draw at Plymouth that featured another strike by Elliott.

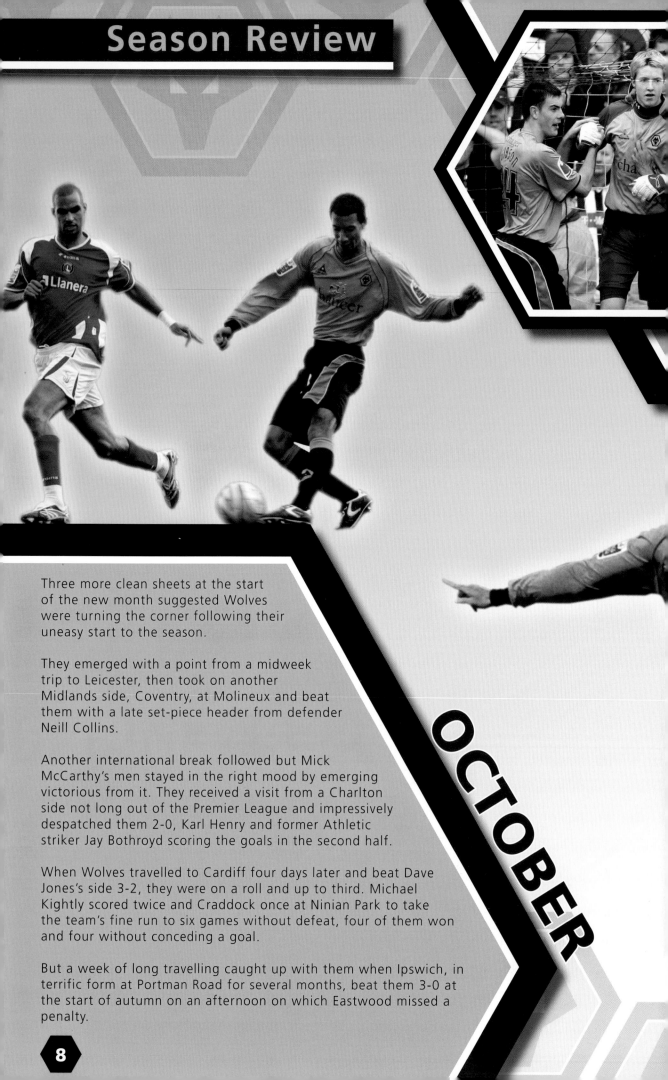

Three more clean sheets at the start of the new month suggested Wolves were turning the corner following their uneasy start to the season.

They emerged with a point from a midweek trip to Leicester, then took on another Midlands side, Coventry, at Molineux and beat them with a late set-piece header from defender Neill Collins.

Another international break followed but Mick McCarthy's men stayed in the right mood by emerging victorious from it. They received a visit from a Charlton side not long out of the Premier League and impressively despatched them 2-0, Karl Henry and former Athletic striker Jay Bothroyd scoring the goals in the second half.

When Wolves travelled to Cardiff four days later and beat Dave Jones's side 3-2, they were on a roll and up to third. Michael Kightly scored twice and Craddock once at Ninian Park to take the team's fine run to six games without defeat, four of them won and four without conceding a goal.

But a week of long travelling caught up with them when Ipswich, in terrific form at Portman Road for several months, beat them 3-0 at the start of autumn on an afternoon on which Eastwood missed a penalty.

OCTOBER

Bristol City, like Wolves, were up in the leading pack and had Michael McIndoe in their line-up in an entertaining 1-1 Molineux draw in which Bothroyd drew first blood.

It was then back on the road for a side who had McIndoe's replacement Matt Jarvis finally nearing fitness after an injury that had plagued him for many weeks. The summer signing figured from the bench in the 0-0 draw at Southampton and was an unused substitute when Collins' goal saw off visiting Barnsley the following Saturday.

Fifth place was a promising platform for Wolves and they made light of the 15-day international break that followed by playing well in the first Black Country derby of the season, Hennessey's late penalty save from Zoltan Gera keeping the scoreline goalless at The Hawthorns. Wolves had to ride their luck to build on the point, an Elliott goal seeing off struggling Colchester at Molineux and taking them up another place to fourth.

NOVEMBER

DECEMBER

All season to date, Wolves had found trouble in winning comfortable-looking games at home and the pattern continued when lowly Preston were beaten only by Henry's second-half strike on the first day of the new month.

Although third place had been reclaimed, performances had taken a down-turn, a point underlined three days later with a defeat at struggling Barnsley. And when Wolves needed a boost in front of the live cameras, they were instead outgunned by an in-form Burnley side at Molineux. Elliott and on-loan Manchester United midfielder Darron Gibson netted but three were conceded at the other end in a second successive defeat.

After a 0-0 draw at QPR, Wolves returned home to contest another low-scoring draw, this time with Leicester, and had again made poor use of games against struggling opponents. The attempt at a much-needed improvement was even more disappointing, with a Boxing Day trip to Hull ending in a 2-0 defeat. Wolves had become desperately short of goals and, although Andy Keogh's third of the season put them ahead at Carrow Road in the last game of 2007, Norwich hit back for a draw that left their visitors only ninth.

Wolves fired more blanks when held by Sheffield United on New Year's Day before being embarrassed by non-League Cambridge United at Molineux four days later. The visitors led deep in the second half of the FA Cup third-round tie, only for Kightly to take some crumbs of comfort from an injury-ravaged winter by scoring one and making one after stepping off the subs' bench.

Steve Morgan was proving true to his word as Sir Jack Hayward's successor by continuing to back Mick McCarthy, who was able to recruit Sylvan Ebanks-Blake and David Edwards in the January transfer window, to be followed by George Elokobi and the on-loan Kevin Kyle. Although Ebanks-Blake's Molineux career started with a 3-0 defeat at home to Crystal Palace, it quickly took off as he scored, along with the debutant Edwards, in the 2-0 victory at Scunthorpe the following weekend. It was Wolves' first win in nine Championship games and proved to be a turning point. A week later, the side ran out resounding 4-1 winners at Watford in the FA Cup, with Keogh's two goals supported by one each from Elliott and Bothroyd.

When Ebanks-Blake's last-minute strike saw off Sheffield Wednesday in a midweek Molineux clash in which Keogh also again scored, Wolves were back among the goals and points in a big way, although they remained rooted in tenth spot.

A quirk of the fixture list saw to it that Wolves had to visit Watford for a second Saturday running. This time it was in the League and there was a different outcome altogether as they crashed 3-0.

Once more, they leaked goals too easily seven days later when Stoke visited Molineux and ran out 4-2 winners, a rare goal by Rob Edwards and one from the in-form Keogh not proving enough.

A 0-0 midweek draw at Blackpool in which Elokobi made his debut stopped the rot but Wolves were then poor in losing 2-0 in the FA Cup fifth round away to Cardiff, who would play twice at Wembley in the competition a few weeks later.

Three points were urgently required and they came at Selhurst Park, where stunning late goals by Gray and Kyle saw off Crystal Palace and ensured Wolves ended another month in tenth place.

MARCH

Lifted by ending their four-match run without a victory, Wolves built on the foundations by winning at Colchester on the first day of the new month. Ebanks-Blake's goal was the only one of the game and three more points would have followed if the side hadn't yielded a last-minute equaliser to Southampton on a night when Ebanks-Blake had struck twice at the right end of Molineux.

There was another blip, in the shape of a 2-1 midweek defeat at Preston, before Wolves really started to click. Keogh's goal at Deepdale was followed by efforts from Seyi Olofinjana, Gray and Ebanks-Blake in a convincing victory back up the M6 at Burnley, then Gray again and Collins secured victory at home to Scunthorpe after a rearranged game had appeared to be going the strugglers' way.

At last Wolves had broken out of mid-table and were eighth – a position they stayed in when battling back well for a high-scoring home draw against QPR, Keogh (2) and Ebanks-Blake the marksmen. Goals were now in rich supply and three more were plundered in a thrilling Saturday teatime visit to Charlton, where Henry struck a dramatic last-minute decider after another Ebanks-Blake brace had set up the victory chance. The door to the play-offs was widening....

APRIL

April was 12 days old before Wolves kicked their first ball in it. They played well, too, in a 0-0 draw at high-riding Bristol City and then had their moments when falling victim by the only goal of the night at Molineux to one of Albion's best performances of the season.

Once more the side's task had become tougher but would have looked less so had they not conceded right at the end after Ebanks-Blake had given them a 73rd minute lead at home to play-off rivals Ipswich.

Three points were essential when FA Cup finalists Cardiff visited Molineux three nights later and they were pocketed safely enough as Keogh, Ebanks-Blake and the fit-again Kightly scored to have the game won within an hour.

Wolves were still two points outside the play-off frame and sensed they needed to win their final two matches to stand any chance of a top-six finish. Victory deserted them at Coventry, though, despite Ebanks-Blake's equaliser from a penalty and it was results elsewhere that kept the dream alive.

To reach the play-offs, Wolves HAD to win their final game – against Plymouth at Molineux – and hope that either Crystal Palace slipped up at home to Burnley or Watford lost at Blackpool.

For a long while on a tense Sunday afternoon, it seemed McCarthy's men would not be able to keep their side of the 'deal.' Then, with 87 minutes gone, Olofinjana, who had scored the club's first goal of the season, also came up with their last.

It was enough to bring a 1-0 win over Argyle but Watford hung on for a draw with ten men at Blackpool, with Palace already far out of sight in their slaughter of Burnley. The combination of results meant Wolves cruelly missed sixth place only on goal difference and had to recharge their batteries in time for another challenge in 2008-09.

MAY

IT'S A FACT

2007-08 milestones
(Coca-Cola Championship unless stated)

- Highest home attendance: 27,883 v West Bromwich Albion on April 15

- Lowest home attendance: 9,625 v Bradford City (Carling Cup) on August 15

- Highest away attendance: 27,992 v Coventry on April 26

- Lowest away attendance: 5,989 v Colchester on March 1

- Biggest win: 4-1 v Watford away (FA Cup) on January 26; 3-0 v Cardiff home on April 22

- Biggest defeat: 3-0 v Ipswich away on October 27, 3-0 v Crystal Palace home on January 12, 3-0 v Watford away on February 2

DEBUTANTS

- Michael Gray, Darren Ward, Stephen Elliott v Watford home on August 11;

- Graham Stack, Freddy Eastwood, Kevin Foley, Elliott Bennett v Bradford City home (Carling Cup) on August 15;

- Matt Jarvis and Darron Gibson v Charlton home on October 20; Sylvan Ebanks-Blake v Crystal Palace home on January 12;

- David Edwards v Scunthorpe away on January 19; Kevin Kyle v Watford away on February 2; George Elokobi v Blackpool away on February 12

FIXTURES 08/09

Date	Time		Opponent	
Sat 9 August	15.00	A	Plymouth	FLC
Sat 16 August	15.00	A	Sheffield Wed	FLC
Sat 23 August	15.00	H	Ipswich Town	FLC
Sat 30 August	15.00	A	Nottm Forest	FLC
Sat 13 September	15.00	H	Charlton	FLC
Tue 16 September	19.45	A	Crystal Palace	FLC
Sat 20 September	15.00	H	Preston	FLC
Sat 27 September	15.00	A	Bristol City	FLC
Tue 30 September	19.45	H	Reading	FLC
Sat 4 October	15.00	H	Swansea City	FLC
Sat 18 October	15.00	A	Coventry City	FLC
Tue 21 October	19.45	H	Norwich City	FLC
Sat 25 October	15.00	A	Watford	FLC
Tue 28 October	19.45	A	Swansea City	FLC
Sat 1 November	15.00	H	Cardiff City	FLC
Sat 8 November	15.00	A	Burnley	FLC
Sat 15 November	15.00	A	Southampton	FLC
Sat 22 November	15.00	H	Blackpool	FLC
Tue 25 November	19.45	A	Sheffield Utd	FLC
Sat 29 November	15.00	A	Birmingham	FLC
Sat 6 December	15.00	H	QPR	FLC
Tue 9 December	19.45	A	Derby County	FLC
Sat 13 December	15.00	H	Barnsley	FLC
Sat 20 December	15.00	A	Doncaster	FLC
Fri 26 December	15.00	H	Sheffield Utd	FLC
Sun 28 December	15.00	A	Blackpool	FLC
Sat 10 January	15.00	H	Preston	FLC
Sat 17 January	15.00	A	Bristol City	FLC
Tue 27 January	19.45	A	Reading	FLC
Sat 31 January	15.00	H	Watford	FLC
Tue 3 Feburary	19.45	A	Norwich City	FLC
Sat 7 Feburary	15.00	A	Coventry City	FLC
Sat 14 Feburary	15.00	H	Burnley	FLC
Sat 21 February	15.00	A	Cardiff City	FLC
Sat 28 Feburary	15.00	H	Plymouth	FLC
Tue 3 March	19.45	A	Crystal Palace	FLC
Sat 7 March	15.00	A	Sheffield Wed	FLC
Tue 10 March	19.45	H	Ipswich Town	FLC
Sat 14 March	15.00	A	Charlton	FLC
Sat 21 March	15.00	H	Nottm Forest	FLC
Sat 4 April	15.00	A	Birmingham	FLC
Sat 11 April	15.00	A	Southampton	FLC
Mon 13 April	19.45	H	Derby County	FLC
Sat 18 April	15.00	A	QPR	FLC
Sat 25 April	15.00	H	Barnsley	FLC
Sun 3 May	15.00	A	Doncaster	FLC

Golden Boy

Sylvan Ebanks-Blake

Sylvan Ebanks-Blake has looked perfectly at home in the famous gold and black – now he has some footwear to match.

Actually, the Golden Boot that came his way as reward for scoring more goals than anyone else in last season's Championship is one to sit in his cabinet at home rather than on his foot. But the cherished prize is another reminder that Wolverhampton Wanderers have a lethal, power-packed striker in their ranks after successfully doing business with Plymouth Argyle over his signature last January. Ebanks-Blake had scored 13 times for the Devon club in the first half of 2007-08 and followed up with 12 for Wolves in the remaining four months to finish with 25 goals for the season.

It meant he pipped West Brom's Kevin Phillips and Sheffield United's James Beattie to the award that put him in good heart for his first full season at Molineux in 2008-09.

"Obviously, I'm delighted with the honour, although it would have meant even more if we had managed to reach the play-offs," said the 22-year-old.

"You hope you are going to settle in quickly with a club but you are never quite sure and it helped me that I scored one or two for Wolves very early on."

"Although I didn't set myself any targets, I did have it in mind in the last few weeks of the season that it would be nice to win the Golden Boot as some very good players have won it in the past and strikers like Kevin Phillips and James Beattie were chasing me in the spring."

"But my bigger aim is to help Wolves to win promotion and hopefully we will be in the Premier League sooner rather than later."

Ebanks-Blake has already had a brief taste of the big time he hopes to be experiencing again soon. Although born in Cambridge and a supporter of Liverpool, his first opportunity in the game was given to him by Manchester United.

" ...my bigger aim is to help Wolves win promotion...

...we have a lot of young, hungry players who are going to get better and better..."

In one of his two senior appearances for Sir Alex Ferguson's team, he scored against Barnet in the Carling Cup but also sat on the bench as an unused substitute in Champions League matches against the likes of Fenerbahce and Lille.

As if trying to compete for a place alongside the likes of Ruud Van Nistelrooy, Wayne Rooney, Ole Gunnar Solksjaer and Luis Saha wasn't difficult enough, though, Sylvan suffered a broken leg towards the end of 2004-05.

While still on the books at Old Trafford, he also had a prolific spell with United's Belgian feeder club, Royal Antwerp, and scored a hat-trick in the Reds reserves before being sold to Plymouth in time for his Argyle debut at home to Wolves on the first day of the 2006-07 season.

No longer is there the same mystery about what he's capable of at first-team level and Wolves fans very quickly took to him.

With seven goals in seven games in March, he won the Powerade Player of the Month award and the last of those, in a thrilling televised 3-2 victory at Charlton, was voted the best of the club's season.

That spectacular finish came on his 22nd birthday and provided another mouth-watering example of the explosive shooting power contained in those feet!

Inevitably, Premier League clubs, including Everton, have already taken a good look at him but he is happy at Wolves and said of his and his side's immediate future: "We fancy our chances."

"We have a lot of young, hungry players who are going to get better and better. It is a very exciting time for everyone connected with Wolverhampton Wanderers."

My Favourite Things

ANDY KEOGH
Holiday destination: Dublin
Other team: Celtic
All-time footballer: Ronaldo (the Brazilian one)

NEILL COLLINS
Holiday destination: Florida
Other team: Kilmarnock
All-time footballer: Eric Cantona

GEORGE ELOKOBI
Holiday destination: Cameroon
Other team: Manchester United
All-time footballer: Maradona

THE BENNETT BOY

From Telford to Japan to senior first-team football, it has been a long journey for Elliott Bennett.

But the winner of Wolverhampton Wanderers' 2008 Young Professional of the Year award hopes he has much further to travel yet.

The 19-year-old, now into his second season as a professional at the club, is one of the many Wolves cubs being tipped for a future that's golden in more ways than one.

And he showed by making his senior debut for no fewer than three clubs in 2007-08 that he is on the right track.

Bennett, whose younger brother Kyle is also on the Wolves books, was given his first opportunity at the top level by being named in Mick McCarthy's starting line-up for the Carling Cup ties at home to Bradford City and Morecambe at the start of last season.

He then played 11 games for Crewe Alexandra and 19 for Bury, scoring a fine goal for both, when loaned out into the lower divisions and is now hoping to gain a stronger foothold in Wolves' first-team squad this term.

"Elliott is a model professional in terms of his dedication, commitment and attitude," said Wolves Assistant Academy Manager John Perkins. "He is a pleasure to work with and we couldn't be more pleased at having him here."

"Crewe were particularly impressed with him and would like to have had him for a bit longer but we have high hopes for him and it was felt right to bring him back here for a while before he went off to Bury instead for a few months."

"Kyle has great ability, too, and we hope he can follow in his brother's footsteps."
The Bennett boys are from Leegomery in Telford and attended the same school that Rob
Edwards had been to a few years earlier. So where does Japan come in?

Well, standing proudly in the Academy offices at the Sir Jack Hayward Training Ground is
a picture of a then tiny Elliott holding aloft the trophy after Wolves had won the under-
12 Shizuoka international competition at one of the venues the country used when
jointly hosting the World Cup with South Korea the following year.
Kyle, also a midfielder, has since been to the same tournament with the club and has
played for England under-18s.

He should have taken inspiration from his older brother being named as the club's Young
Pro of the Year – further proof of the outstanding sporting talent which has in addition
seen him represent Shropshire at the All England Schools Athletics Championships and
been county age-group champion in a couple of events.

Remember how the likes of Wayne Hennessey and Matt Murray went out on loan to
the less glamorous end of the Football League before making it really big at Molineux?
Maybe, just maybe, another huge star is in the making among the likes of Bennett and
the other Wolves lads who have gone out to lower-division clubs in the last few months.

"We didn't use Elliott in our FA Youth Cup side last season, as we could have done,
because it was considered to be more beneficial for him to be playing in somebody else's
first team," Perkins added. "Nor did we take him on tour in the summer. He has learned
more doing what he has done."

ELLIOTT BENNETT

SAM VOKES

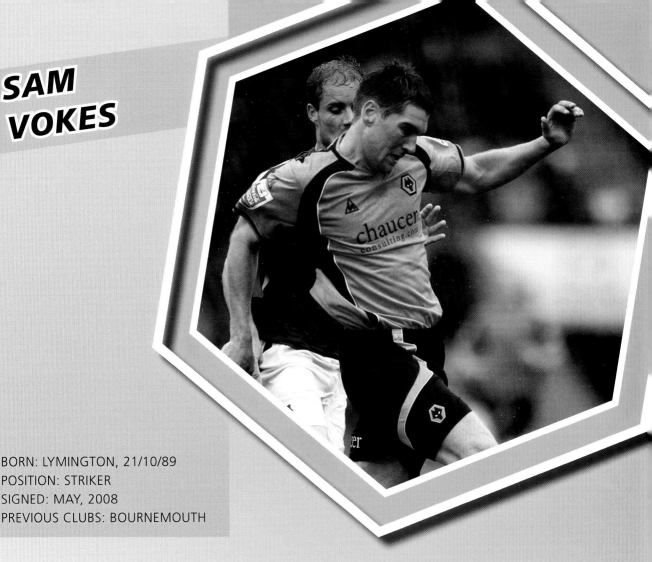

BORN: LYMINGTON, 21/10/89
POSITION: STRIKER
SIGNED: MAY, 2008
PREVIOUS CLUBS: BOURNEMOUTH

Last season had barely ended by the time Mick McCarthy swooped to make Sam Vokes his first signing of the summer.

The Wolves manager makes a habit of seeking out up-and-coming young players in the transfer market – and the six-foot-plus forward is no different.

He is not 20 until late next year but has already shown his potential by building on his Welsh under-21 caps by playing twice for the senior team – in the friendlies away to Iceland and Holland shortly before Euro 2008.

Vokes, who had also been linked with Celtic, Newcastle and Aston Villa, suffered the disappointment of relegation from League One with Bournemouth in the spring. But he still scored 12 goals for them in 2007-08, including braces at home to both Nottingham Forest and Hartlepool, and also netted four times the previous season.

He got off the mark for Wolves in the victory against Kilmarnock on the pre-season tour of Scotland and said about his move to the Championship: "I was flattered when I heard of Wolves' interest."

"They are always at the top end of the Championship and a club of this size deserves to be in the Premier League. The facilities and ground are great."

Vokes, signed for an undisclosed fee, is on a four-year contract, having totalled 16 goals in his 59 Bournemouth matches.

NEW SIGNINGS

RICHARD STEARMAN

BORN: WOLVERHAMPTON, 19/08/87
POSITION: DEFENDER
SIGNED: JUNE, 2008
PREVIOUS CLUBS: LEICESTER

Wolves wouldn't have had the chance to sign Richard Stearman from Leicester had it not been for the vision of one of their former players and coaches.

The young defender was wanted by Sunderland when Rob Kelly was manager of Leicester – but the ex-Molineux man decided to hang on to a player he thought would get better and better.

He was proved right. Stearman was named as Leicester's Player of the Year at the end of their 2007-08 relegation season and was signed a few weeks later by Mick McCarthy. He had earlier been crowned as their Young Player of the Year, having made his first-team debut against Cardiff in October, 2004 at the age of only 17.

Now 21, Stearman showed in his 130 games for the East Midlanders that he can play at right-back or centre-half and has already done enough to impress those in international football.

He has played for England under-17s and under-19s and went into this season hoping to make his under-21 debut after being called up last season without making it past the substitutes' bench.

Moving to Wolves was special for him as he is from the city. "I lived in Wightwick until I was five, so I have got a fair few members of my family around here and my grandparents only recently left the area," he said.

NEW SIGNINGS

DAVID JONES

BORN: SOUTHPORT, 04/11/84
POSITION: MIDFIELDER
SIGNED: JUNE, 2008
PREVIOUS CLUBS: MANCHESTER
UNITED, PRESTON (LOAN),
NEC NIJMEGEN (LOAN), DERBY

Wolves last won promotion under the management of a Dave Jones. Now they have a David Jones on their playing staff who knows what it's like to graduate to the Premier League.

This summer giving a three-year contract to a left-footer Mick McCarthy believes will bring balance to his midfield, Wolves have a relative youngster who went up via the play-offs with Derby in May, 2007.

And there's good breeding there, too, because this Jones learned his trade at Manchester United and played four games in Sir Alex Ferguson's first team before being sold for £1m.

Sylvan Ebanks-Blake arrived at Wolves by a similar route and was delighted to welcome aboard an old team-mate from Old Trafford. Jones also has England under-21 honours and was delighted to move hot on the heels of Richard Stearman from the East Midlands to the West Midlands.

"Wolves are a traditional football club which all the staff are geared into and that suits me down to the ground," he said on his arrival.

"I think this is the right stage for me to push on and progress my career."

Jones has a useful scoring record that Wolves will be keen to develop in their own efforts to escape from the Championship.

NEW SIGNINGS

CHRIS IWELUMO

BORN: COATBRIDGE, 01/08/78
POSITION: STRIKER
SIGNED: JULY, 2008
PREVIOUS CLUBS: ST MIRREN,
AARHUS, PRESTON, STOKE, YORK
(LOAN), CHELTENHAM (LOAN),
BRIGHTON (LOAN), ALEMANIA,
COLCHESTER, CHARLTON

The term 'well-travelled' might have been designed with players like Chris Iwelumo in mind.

The second summer addition to Wolves' striker ranks has certainly spread his wings far and wide from his Scottish roots, having two spells abroad as well as no fewer than eight clubs in England.

And, having developed a decent scoring record at Stoke, it was his goals at Colchester that marked him out as one to watch.

He netted no fewer than 37 times in 103 games for the Essex side and was successful enough to persuade newly-relegated Charlton to take him on in the summer of last year. Now it's at Wolves that he is aiming to give defenders a hard time and the impact he

made on the three-match tour of his native Scotland went some way to making him an immediate favourite.

At the age of 29 at the time of his signing, the Scotland B international is a shade older than most of Mick McCarthy's other captures at Molineux.

"Maybe I will bring that bit of experience but I'm not sure that's necessarily needed," he said. "There are some very good strikers here. It's a fantastic club and hopefully I will bring something to the table."

NEW SIGNINGS

JODY CRADDOCK
Position: Defender
Born: Redditch, 25/7/75
Signed: July, 2003
Other clubs: Cambridge United, Sunderland, Sheffield United (loan), Stoke (loan)

Jody Craddock: His Molineux days seemed to be numbered when he was loaned to Stoke last autumn but he bounced back to reclaim a regular place at Wolves and prove his manager Mick McCarthy wrong. One of Wolves' longest-serving players.

DARREN WARD
Position: Defender
Born: London, 13/9/78
Signed: July, 2007
Other clubs: Watford, QPR (loan), Millwall, Crystal Palace

Darren Ward: Had a mixed first Molineux season that ended with him being transfer-listed despite playing 32 games. Had previously spent his entire career in the London area and played in an FA Cup final for Millwall.

DAVID EDWARDS

Position: Midfielder
Born: Shrewsbury, 3/2/86
Signed: January, 2008
Other clubs: Shrewsbury, Luton

David Edwards: Signed by Wolves after impressing for Luton in their FA Cup epic against Liverpool last winter. In a memorable but ultimately injury-hit 2007/08 campaign, he made his senior debut for Wales and scored on his Wanderers debut.

FREDDY EASTWOOD

Position: Forward
Born: Basildon, 29/10/83
Signed: July, 2007
Other clubs: West Ham, Grays Athletic, Sunderland (loan), Southend

Freddy Eastwood: Remained a popular figure with fans throughout 2007/08 despite failing to secure anything like a regular place. Started well at the club but his only goals after August were for Wales and he was transfer-listed in the summer.

SYLVAN EBANKS-BLAKE

Position: Forward
Born: Cambridge, 29/3/86
Signed: January, 2008
Other clubs: Manchester United, Royal Antwerp (loan), Plymouth

Sylvan Ebanks-Blake: Enjoyed a tremendous four months at Molineux and brought his Plymouth form to the West Midlands, winning the Golden Boot as the Championship's top scorer and almost shooting Wolves into the play-offs.

STEPHEN ELLIOT
Position: Forward
Born: Dublin, 6/1/84
Signed: July, 2008
Other clubs: Manchester City, Sunderland

Stephen Elliott: Had a quiet first season at Molineux – one containing five goals and also a few injury problems. His 31 appearances in 2007/08 contained 12 as a substitute and he was another transfer-listed early in the close season.

GEORGE ELOKOBI
Position: Defender
Born: Cameroon, 31/1/86
Signed: January, 2008
Other clubs: Colchester, Chester (loan)

George Elokobi: Made a good impression after being signed in mid-season and became a regular at left-back. He was rated by his manager as one of the very best in his position in the Championship and is another only in his early 20s.

KEVIN FOLEY
Position: Defender
Born: Luton, 1/11/84
Signed: August, 2007
Other club: Luton

Kevin Foley: Quickly looked at home when introduced as Mick McCarthy's preferred right-back early in 2007/08 and hardly missed a game from then on. He also remains on the fringes of the senior Republic of Ireland side.

MICHAEL GRAY

Position: Utility man
Born: Sunderland, 3/8/74
Signed: July, 2007
Other clubs: Sunderland, Celtic (loan), Blackburn, Leeds (loan)

Michael Gray: Appeared to have been signed as left-back cover but produced his best form of 2007/08 in midfield and had a useful run of goal-scoring. Has played around 550 games in his career but still very energetic.

WAYNE HENNESSEY

Position: Goalkeeper
Born: Anglesey, 24/1/87
Signed: April, 2005
Other clubs: Bristol City (loan), Stockport (loan)

Wayne Hennessey: Has made fabulous strides from being a young stand-by to a regular choice both for Wolves and his country Wales. Won a cluster of Player of the Year awards in 2008 and clearly has a wonderful future in the game.

KARL HENRY

Position: Midfielder
Born: Wolverhampton, 26/11/82
Signed: August, 2006
Other clubs: Stoke, Cheltenham (loan)

Karl Henry: Has already acquired substantial captaincy experience in his Wolves career and, as befitting a player who has always supported the club, continues to give his all for them. Also the scorer of some valuable goals.

MATT JARVIS
Position: Midfielder
Born: Middlesbrough, 22/5/86
Signed: June, 2007
Other clubs: Millwall, Gillingham

Matt Jarvis: Was desperately unlucky with injuries after being signed as Michael McIndoe's replacement but showed signs of his potential later in his debut season. Could form an exciting wing partnership with Michael Kightly.

ANDY KEOGH
Position: Forward
Born: Dublin, 16/5/86
Signed: January, 2007
Other clubs: Leeds, Bury (loan), Scunthorpe

Andy Keogh: After his excellent form of 2006/07, had a quieter first half to 2007/08 before then regaining his goal-scoring edge. Has also continued his emergence with the Republic of Ireland by netting for them, too.

MICHAEL KIGHTLY
Position: Midfielder
Born: Basildon, 24/1/86
Signed: November, 2006 (initially on loan)
Other clubs: Southend, Farnborough (loan), Grays Athletic

Michael Kightly: Another to suffer bad luck with injuries in 2007/08 and was ruled out of England under-21 action against Poland at Molineux. Was playing superbly when he went out of the side in November and didn't return until the spring.

MATT MURRAY

Position: Goalkeeper
Born: Solihull, 2/5/81
Signed: August, 1997
Other clubs: Tranmere (loan), Slough
(loan), Kingstonian (loan)

Matt Murray: Missed the entire 2007/08
campaign through a knee injury – not the
first time that has happened in his stop-
start Molineux career. Now facing a battle
with Wayne Hennessey to establish himself
as the No. 1 keeper.

NEILL COLLINS

Position: Defender
Born: Irvine, Scotland, 2/9/83
Signed: November, 2006 (initially on loan)
Other clubs: Queens Park, Dumbarton,
Sunderland, Hartlepool (loan), Sheffield
United (loan)

Neill Collins: Showed a flair for coming
up with useful set-piece goals – and
valuable late ones at that – as Wolves fell
agonisingly short of the play-offs. Also
continues to demonstrate an ability to
play anywhere in defence.

SEYI OLOFINJANA

Position: Midfielder
Born: Lagos, 30/6/80
Signed: July, 2004
Other clubs: Crown Ogbosomo, Kwara
United, Brann Bergen

Seyi Olofinjana: Was unable to reproduce
his terrific scoring form of 2006/07 but
has still been a Wolves regular despite
departing to play for Nigeria in the
African Cup of Nations in January. Scored
on the first and last days of 2007/08.

STEPHEN WARD
Position: Forward
Born: Dublin, 20/8/85
Signed: January, 2007
Other club: Bohemians

Stephen Ward: Has seen the goals dry up after a bright scoring start to his Wolves career, although he has had injuries and also been asked to play a different role wide on the left for a lengthy spell in the absence of Matt Jarvis.

STEPHEN GLEESON
Position: Midfielder
Born: Dublin, 3/8/88
Signed: July, 2005
Other clubs: Stockport (loan), Hereford (loan)

Stephen Gleeson: Used only once by Wolves in 2007/08 but had two loan spells in League Two, the second at Stockport, who he had also served the previous year and who he helped to promotion by scoring in the play-off semi-final at Wycombe.

MARK DAVIES
Position: Midfielder
Born: Wolverhampton, 10/2/88
Signed: August, 2005
Other clubs: None

Mark Davies: Didn't figure at all in 2007/08 after also missing virtually all of 2006/07 through injury and is looking to resurrect his career after the bright form under Glenn Hoddle that suggested he was a big star of the future.

MARK LITTLE

Position: Defender
Born: Worcester, 20/8/88
Signed: August, 2005
Other clubs: Northampton (loan)

Mark Little: Made only one senior
appearance for Wolves in 2007/08
following more than 30 the previous
season but continued his football
education with an extended loan spell at
Northampton. In three months at Sixfields,
he played 17 games.

PLAYER FILES

My Favourite Things

KARL HENRY
Holiday destination: Nevada (USA)
Other team: There is no other team – I always supported Wolves!
All-time footballer: Alan Shearer

SYLVAN EBANKS-BLAKE
Holiday destination: Marbella (Spain)
Other team: Liverpool
All-time footballer: Andy Cole

MICHAEL KIGHTLY
Holiday destination: Dubai
Other team: Tottenham
All-time footballer: David Ginola

Jobs for the Girls
Wolves supporter and Match of the Day commentator Jacqui Oatley

England and the other home countries may have been missing from this summer's European Championship finals but Austria and Switzerland did contain a little Wolverhampton quarter for two or three weeks.

In the absence of any British representation on the field, the main participants from these shores were a handful of supporters and members of the media 'army.'

And the latter contingent contained former Wolves apprentice Stan Collymore and another well-known BBC 5 Live voice, Jacqui Oatley. Jacqui, born in Wolverhampton and brought up in Codsall, is frequently heard reading sports bulletins on the station and, as well as reporting on games at grounds up and down the country during the English season, commentates on matches for 5 Live and Sports Extra.

Her biggest claim to fame, though, is her emergence as the first-ever female commentator on BBC TV's Match of the Day – an honour that came her way when she was handed the microphone for the Fulham v Blackburn clash in April, 2007. And it was the small screen that took much of her time at the Euro 2008 tournament, as she found herself interviewing the likes of Michael Ballack, Cesc Fabregas and Fernando Torres.

"I had a roving sort of role, sending reports and interviews from the various cities and grounds for different programmes," said the former pupil of St Dominic's, Brewood, and Wolverhampton Grammar School. "They included the live shows, highlights shows, Football Focus and the internet. I also wrote a blog for the BBC website giving some of the background to what went on behind the scenes."

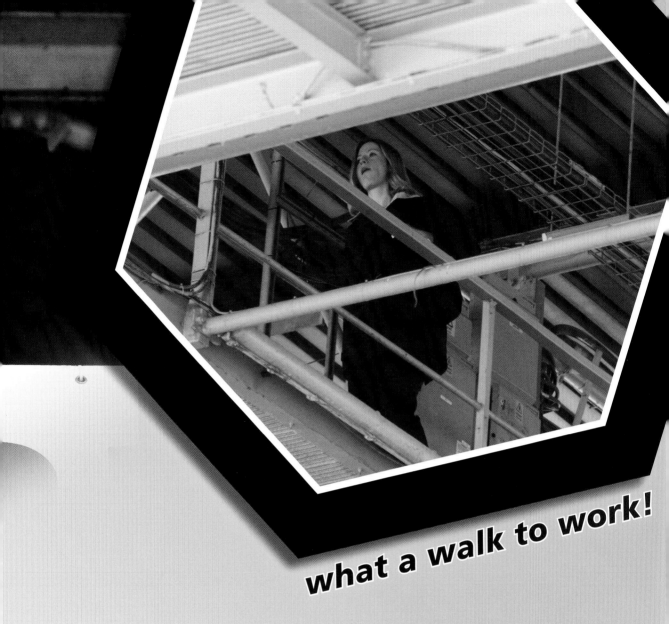

what a walk to work!

"I went to the women's World Cup in China near the start of the season which involved plenty of travelling, so that prepared me well for this trip. But it was terrific to be part of a major tournament and sample the incredible atmosphere you get at big events like this, even if it was disappointing that neither England nor any of the other home countries were there."

"I studied German at university and it came in really useful in Austria, which is where I was based. I was able to read the newspapers over there to keep up to date with what was going on."

Jacqui, who herself played football before suffering a serious knee injury, left Wolverhampton in the early 1990s to go to university in Leeds, but still returns to her roots whenever possible to catch up with family and friends. She now lives in London.

She was also back in town at the start of May to act as MC at Wolves' Player of the Year awards night at Wolverhampton's Park Hall Hotel and hopes it won't be long before the Beeb are descending in numbers again on Molineux as a Premier League venue.

"Working for the BBC is all about remaining neutral and you can't allow any old loyalties to get in the way of work," she added. "But it would be great for the Premier League to have a club the size of Wolves in it, bearing in mind its wonderful history and tradition. It would also be fantastic for the city of Wolverhampton to have its club being talked about in the national and international media. After getting there it's all about staying there, and becoming established as a top-flight club again would do wonders for the city."

Keeping Standards High

Wolves goalkeeper coach Bobby Mimms talking about Wolves goalkeeping stars such as Matt Murray and Wayne Hennessey

No-one knows Wolves' talented keepers better than the man who served for seven years as the club's goalkeeper coach, Bobby Mimms – and he thinks they're absolutely golden! Mimms, himself a talented former last line of defence with the likes of Blackburn Rovers, Everton, Tottenham Hotspur and at international level with England under-21s, is perfectly placed to sum up the riches at the disposal of the management at Molineux. Which is why he has no hesitation in singing the praises of Wayne Hennessey, Matt Murray and their young rival Carl Ikeme.

"Every club in the Championship would love to have what we have in our goalkeeping department and a fair few Premier League clubs as well," he said.

"One for one, there are very few better in the country than what Wolves have. There are some excellent keepers in the top flight but I'm not convinced many sides have the strength in depth that Wolves have in this area of the squad. And the Championship clubs certainly don't."

"Everyone will know Wayne and Matt now but Carl has the potential to be very good as well and we're very pleased to have the three of them."

Mimms, in his mid-40s and brought to Wolves by the club's ex-manager Dave Jones at the end of a playing career of some 20 years, regards himself as a lucky man to have been able to work with such talent before his departure to Blackburn at the start of the season. But Mick McCarthy saw fit to highlight the coach's own contribution to their development when Hennessey last spring followed Murray 12 months earlier in being presented with a host of Player of the Year awards and other honours.

So how do the two of them compare in their approach to the game?

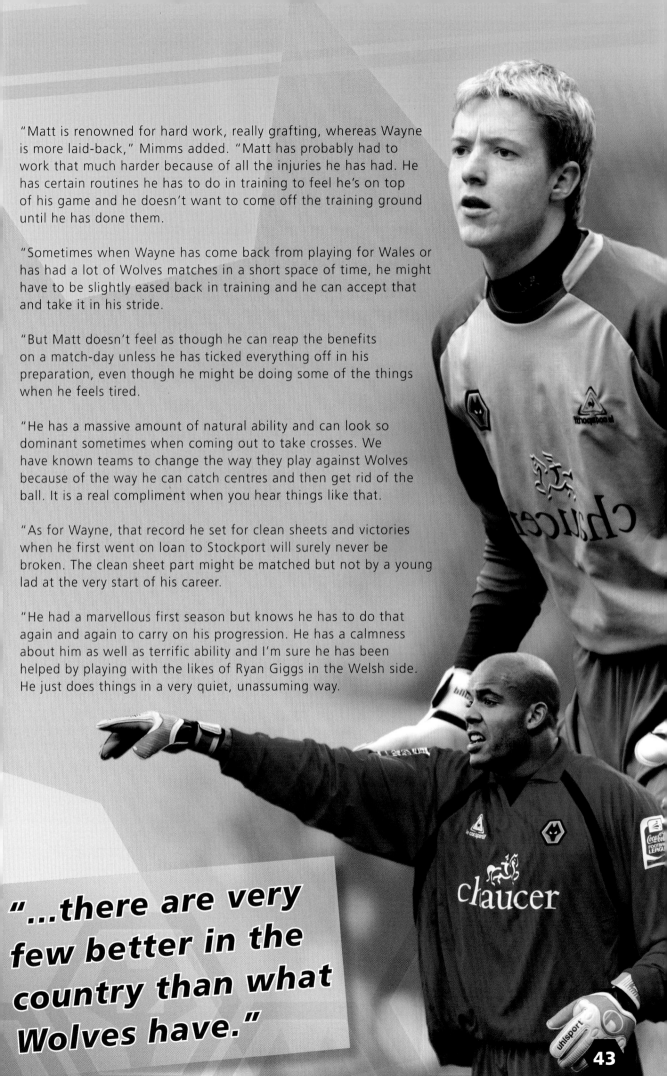

"Matt is renowned for hard work, really grafting, whereas Wayne is more laid-back," Mimms added. "Matt has probably had to work that much harder because of all the injuries he has had. He has certain routines he has to do in training to feel he's on top of his game and he doesn't want to come off the training ground until he has done them.

"Sometimes when Wayne has come back from playing for Wales or has had a lot of Wolves matches in a short space of time, he might have to be slightly eased back in training and he can accept that and take it in his stride.

"But Matt doesn't feel as though he can reap the benefits on a match-day unless he has ticked everything off in his preparation, even though he might be doing some of the things when he feels tired.

"He has a massive amount of natural ability and can look so dominant sometimes when coming out to take crosses. We have known teams to change the way they play against Wolves because of the way he can catch centres and then get rid of the ball. It is a real compliment when you hear things like that.

"As for Wayne, that record he set for clean sheets and victories when he first went on loan to Stockport will surely never be broken. The clean sheet part might be matched but not by a young lad at the very start of his career.

"He had a marvellous first season but knows he has to do that again and again to carry on his progression. He has a calmness about him as well as terrific ability and I'm sure he has been helped by playing with the likes of Ryan Giggs in the Welsh side. He just does things in a very quiet, unassuming way.

"...there are very few better in the country than what Wolves have."

"It is interesting that they differ but they are both very professional in their approach and love to talk about a game afterwards, whether they've won, lost or drawn. There is a little goalkeeper club at Molineux and the lads pull each other along where they can, so that any award won by them is seen as an honour for the group as well as just the individual."

Murray is six years older of the two and had picked up England under-21 honours before Hennessey made his Wolves debut and immediately showed form that not only brought him a chance with the senior Wales team but very quickly saw him established as their No. 1 keeper.

Hennessey's 2007-08 season was as impressive as the one Murray had in 2002-03 when first coming to notice at first-team level and helping Wolves to promotion.

And, if the latter can finally put his cruel catalogue of injuries behind him, they seem set for a major battle for the goalkeeper jersey at Molineux this term.

Not that Mimms has anything other than high hopes also for the 22-year-old Ikeme, another Wolves keeper who has had more than his fair share of injuries.

"He can be very good as well," he added. "What he needs is a kinder run with his fitness and to play some more meaningful games. He has acquitted himself well in the few opportunities he has had and has good influences around him.

"Goalkeepers probably work harder than the outfield players because they will take part in the fitness work and the practice games with them, then they might stay out for some kicking practice. And they might well follow that with some work in the gym to make sure their strength is up.

"Nothing would please me more than seeing all three play in the Premier League for Wolves."

"Goalkeepers probably work harder than the outfield players..."

"Every club in the Championship would love to have what we have in our goalkeeping department and a fair few Premier League clubs as well"

QUIZ : Know your club's season

See how many of these ten questions about Wolves in 2007-08 you can answer correctly.

1. Which forward made his Championship debut for Wolves (and was taken off during the game) against Watford on the first day of the season?

2. Who scored Wolves' goal in the above opening-day fixture?

3. Against which club did Wolves record their first draw of 2007-08?

4. Who did Wolves sign Kevin Foley from?

5. For which country has Michael Gray won three senior international caps?

6. What position were Wolves in the table after they drew at Albion in November, 2007?

7. Which player scored two of Wolves' goals in the 4-1 FA Cup win at Watford in January, 2007?

8. Who is the left-back Wolves signed from Colchester early in 2008?

9. Which Wolves player scored against Crystal Palace, Burnley and Scunthorpe late in the winter?

10. Who scored Wolves' final goal of 2007-08?

46

Answers on page 61.

THE IRISH
CONNECTION

It used to be Scots that poured into English football in big numbers. Now clubs make their signings from all over the world. But, at Wolverhampton Wanderers, no nation is represented more – other than the home country, of course – than the Republic of Ireland. Manager Mick McCarthy, who himself made 57 appearances for the country despite being born and bred in Barnsley, has assembled a squad who are well sprinkled with players from the other side of the Irish Sea.

No fewer than eight members of last season's senior playing staff are either from or qualified to play for the Republic of Ireland; Gary Breen, Andy Keogh, Stephen Ward, Darren Potter, Stephen Gleeson, Stephen Elliott, Kevin Foley and the on-loan Darron Gibson.

It's an amazing collection of players from one relatively small country because Wolves have not had particularly strong links with that part of the world in the past. Until the 1990s, they had had few senior Irish internationals on their books, although they did at one time recruit heavily from the Republic for their Academy.

In the late 1980s and 1990s, though, David Kelly, who had a couple of years at Molineux from 1993 to 1995, did well for a country who were then managed by former England World Cup winner Jack Charlton, then Robbie Keane faced

MICK McCARTHY

ROBBIE KEANE

STEPHEN GLEESON

47

the Czech Republic and Argentina in 1998 at the very start of a magnificent international career that has so far brought him well over 80 matches and 30 goals. Keane is the Republic of Ireland's highest ever goalscorer and has also had considerable captaincy experience with them, his former Molineux colleague David Connolly (on loan from Dutch club Feyenoord) playing alongside him at national level, too.

Mark Kennedy also had a good career with the country of his birth, although most of his 34 caps were picked up while he was playing for clubs prior to his stay at Wolves.
Although McCarthy also had a successful spell as Ireland manager, you have to dig deep to find many connections between the two teams prior to 1990. Goalkeeper Mick Kearns, at Molineux around the time of the 1980 League Cup final win over Nottingham Forest, is one who played in both sides – and Maurice Daly, who was briefly seen at both levels in the late 1970s, is another. And, going further back into Wolves history, full-back Phil Kelly played five times for the Irish in the early 1960s while struggling to make a name for himself as a First Division player under the management of Stan Cullis. He made only 18 Wanderers appearances before leaving for Norwich. Two other players who some young Wolves supporters will have heard of are Dominic Foley and Glen Crowe. Both played a handful of games in the club's attack in the mid and late 1990s and have won a few caps for the Republic since leaving the West Midlands.

So the current glut of Irish voices around the Molineux dressing room is something that has never been heard before. Keogh, Stephen Ward, Potter, Gleeson, Elliott and Gibson were all born on the other side of the water but anyone who has spoken to Breen and Foley will realise that they are both from the London area while a conversation with Potter will quickly reveal that he is from Liverpool! Keogh made an immediate impact on new Irish manager Giovanni Trapattoni when he was sent on as a substitute against Serbia in the Italian's first game in charge last May and equalised with a spectacular goal. He and Ward have at times formed an all-Irish strike-force at Molineux and are just two of the reasons why Wolves fans are likely to follow the results of the other home countries with even keener interest in the coming seasons.

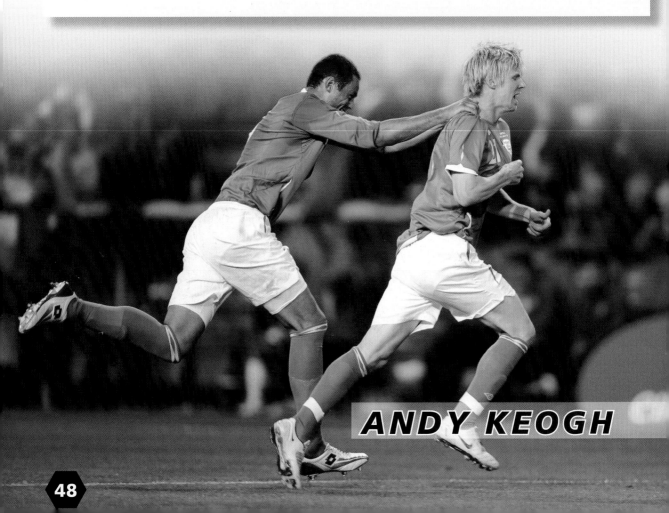

ANDY KEOGH

STEPHEN ELLIOT

ENGLAND EXPECTS

Promotion wasn't the only big aim for Michael Kightly when he entered his second full season as a Wolverhampton Wanderers player in August. He was also hoping for a thrilling end to his England under-21 career with a place in the squad for next summer's European Championships in Sweden.

The Wolves winger made his debut in Stuart Pearce's side against Romania at Bristol City's Ashton Gate in the August of the 2007-08 season and followed up by going on as a substitute for Aston Villa's Gabriel Agbonlahor both in a victory in Bulgaria a few weeks later and in the 1-0 win against Montenegro at Leicester.

Another highlight was due to come his way with the opportunity to face Poland at Molineux in March but he was ruled out by the ankle injury that took a big chunk out of his season.

But any disappointment at missing out on that big 'home' date would be made up for if England, who were due to play home and away play-off games this autumn, are heading for Scandinavia at the end of the current campaign.

Although already having turned 22, Kightly would still able to play in the final stages of Europe's prestige under-21 tournament in a few months' time as he was within the age limit when the qualifying campaign kicked off.
"It would be a big thrill if I could be part of the Championships finals," Kightly said. "It was so disappointing not to be fit for the under-21 international that was staged at Molineux earlier this year, so I'd be delighted to be part of things in the summer.

"England did brilliantly in the last finals in Holland before losing on penalties in the semi-finals and there's a feeling we could challenge strongly again this time.

"Just being there in the squad and taking part would be fabulous for me, so I've got my fingers crossed. Promotion is obviously the big target but the possibility of having some important international football at the end of the season has been another huge target."

Wolves have a host of internationals at various levels in their current squad and also have a proud record of having provided many players down the years for England under-21s.

Keeper Matt Murray and fellow defenders Joleon Lescott and Lee Naylor have all played for the side in the last few seasons, Lescott having since gone on to play several times for the senior team.

And Dean Richards, then a newly-signed Wolves defender, had the massive honour of captaining the team – one containing David Beckham and Phil Neville no less – at the 1995 Toulon Tournament in the south of France.

And, a few years before that, Steve Bull played five times in the side, on one memorable occasion alongside his Wolves strike-partner Andy Mutch – a remarkable feat for a club who were then in the Third Division, or League One as it is now known.

Other England under-21 players (or under-23 internationals as they previously were) produced at Molineux since the early 1970s are Paul Bradshaw, Geoff Palmer, Derek Parkin, Bob Hazell, Kenny Hibbitt, John Richards and Alan Sunderland.

MICHAEL KIGHTLY

JOLEON LESCOTT

MATT MURRAY

PUZZLES

Anagrams

Unravel the letters in the words and names below to come up with ten players who represented Wolves in 2008. Ignore the punctuation, capital letters and occasional spelling mistake!

1. Key VEL info

2. Jam tarts iv

3. Lay rich game

4. Gee, Look! Beg Rio

5. Dvd war is dead

6. e.g. I'm chilly Kath

7. Val sank Lyn's kebab

8. AV smokes

9. Rhyl krane

10. Hog and key

Spot the Ball

Answers on page 61.

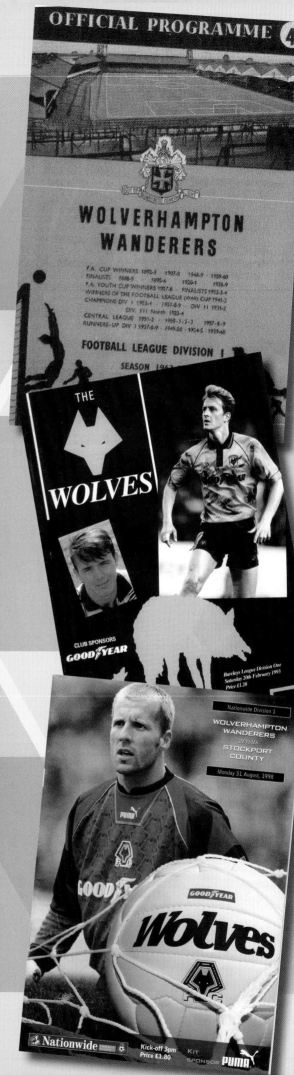

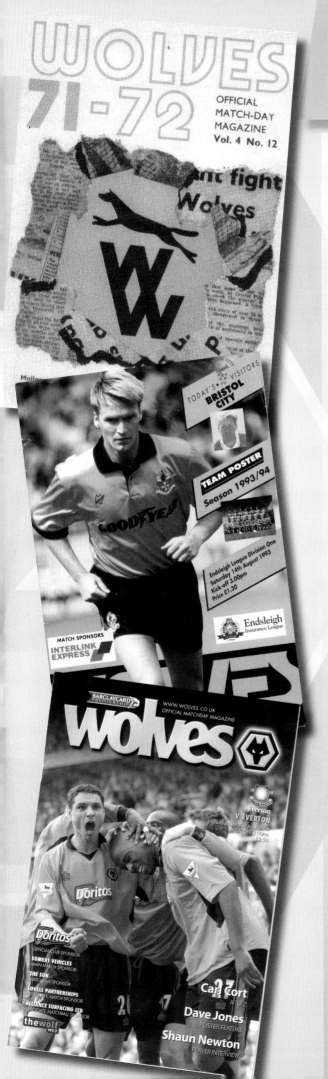

PROGRAMMES DOWN THE YEARS

Football programmes come in different shapes and sizes but all have one thing in common – they should NEVER be thrown away!

Publications that you might think are just for a little light reading before kick-off and at half-time on match-days could eventually become very valuable.

The keen collector would never dream of missing even a single issue from his club's season but, even if you are not able to get your hands on a copy from every match, make sure you save those that come your way.

Lofts and cupboards around the West Midlands must contain thousands and thousands of pounds' worth of old Wolves programmes. Look on ebay and you will see what high prices some rare ones sell for.

It was unusual for programmes to be printed at all for games before the First World War. Then, for years, they were often little more than team sheets. As such, though, they were a vital means of identifying players in the days well before electronic scoreboards and even Tannoy systems. The 1950s and early 1960s version, typified by the one pictured from a match against Fulham with players silhouetted, will be remembered particularly happily by older Wolves fans as this design lasted for many seasons. It was only in the late 1960s that the use of photographs increased as part of a move to a magazine format. Now, programmes are full-colour magazines, containing not only everything you need to know about your team but also various commercial features about your club.

Wolves have won much praise and also some awards for the quality of their match-day publication over the years, so their fans are some of the best informed in the country. All of which should make you think when next wondering whether to buy from those sellers who stand outside Molineux come rain or shine!

QUIZ : Know your club's history

HOW WELL DO YOU KNOW YOUR CLUB?
TEST YOUR KNOWLEDGE ON THESE TEN QUESTIONS
RELATING TO BIG MOMENTS AND EVENTS IN WOLVES' HISTORY.

1. Who is Wolves' all-time record goalscorer?
2. Whose goal record did he overtake in 1992?
3. Which Wolves player played 105 times for England, 70 of those games coming as captain?
4. Who managed Wolves to three League Championship triumphs and the winning of two FA Cups in the club's glory years from 1949-60?
5. In which year did Steve Bull retire as a Wolves player?
6. Which club gave Bully his first chance as a manager in 2008?
7. Which famous former Wolves and Northern Ireland player died on June 24, 2007?
8. Which knockout competition did Wolves win in 1988?
9. Who was the manager when the club won the above competition and the Fourth Division and Third Division titles in 1988 and 1989?
10. Which former England manager did Wolves appoint as their manager in 1994?

Answers on page 61.

JODY CRADDOCK

BILLY WRIGHT

Billy Wright STAND

CAPTAINS' CLUB
An Elite Group

When Jody Craddock or Karl Henry emerges from Molineux's famous players tunnel to lead Wolverhampton Wanderers' side out, they are in illustrious company.

Just consider some of the names who have captained Wolves in the past and you will realise we are talking about an elite group of men......

Stan Cullis, Billy Wright, Mike Bailey, Emlyn Hughes and Paul Ince to name just five.

The quintet are arguably the most famous skippers Wolves have ever had and you can be sure Craddock and Henry are bursting with pride each time they are handed the coveted armband. A good captain, it is said, can raise the performance level of their team a few notches, either with their encouragement or with the way they lead by example.

Who, for instance, would want to be caught slouching when Ince is likely to appear at your side and administer his version of Sir Alex Ferguson's infamous 'hairdryer' treatment! And you would never want to let down a captain who has the respect of the rest of your team-mates. Most of Cullis' playing career was before the Second World War and he had very obvious leadership quality. He first skippered Wolves when he was 19 and officially became club captain in the week of his 20th birthday.

He wasn't finished there, though. He led the Football League in a game against the Scottish League when he was 21 and was named at the age of only 22 as one of England's youngest captains.

Wright's career with club and country is legendary. He was Wolves skipper well before they lifted the FA Cup by beating Leicester at Wembley in 1949 – a position he held until his retirement in 1959 – and no fewer than 70 of

KARL HENRY

MIKE BAILEY

his then record 105 England caps were achieved with him at the head of the team.

Wright was recognised the world over as the perfect gentleman and Bailey had his own big army of admirers after being appointed to the Molineux captaincy a few months after his arrival in 1966.

"Wolves haven't had a better skipper since," says John Richards of the man who drove the Wanderers side on for around a decade. "We all had the utmost respect for him. He was a terrific inspiration to all the players around him."

Bailey, whose own two England caps were won before he left Charlton for Molineux in the year of England's World Cup win, went up Wembley's famous steps first to receive the League Cup in 1974 and says it was a 'shivery' moment when he turned round to show it off to the gold and black hordes.

And Hughes, best known as a Liverpool hero, had the same thrill in 1980 when Wolves unexpectedly beat Brian Clough's Nottingham Forest in the final of the same competition. Wembley success then came eight years later to the team led by Alistair Robertson, a man whose sterling deeds over two title-winning seasons at Molineux brought forgiveness for his many years earlier service with Albion!

Robertson was something of a hard man in the mould of Ince, who was in charge when Wolves unforgettably beat Sheffield United to win the play-off final at the Millennium Stadium in 2003. So the likes of Craddock and Henry have a lot to live up to when they go up to toss the coin with their opposite number. But who knows what sort of glory might be coming their way at the end of the season?

Crowded House: Breaking attendance records

Manchester United may be Champions League and Premier League title holders but how about this for a little-known fact? It won't please the Old Trafford hordes one bit that, despite all the glory years under Sir Alex Ferguson and Sir Matt Busby, the biggest attendance ever to assemble at the ground was not for a United game at all – but one involving Wolves and Grimsby Town!

There was a whopping 76,962 gate to watch Stan Cullis's Wolves hammer Grimsby 5-0 in the semi-final of the 1938-39 FA Cup and, at the start of the 2008-09 season, that figure was almost 900 higher than the biggest crowd United have ever attracted to their Theatre of Dreams – the 76,098 who saw the top-flight game against Blackburn in March, 2007. Wolves were watched by 67,648 on their last visit to Old Trafford five years ago and that was the biggest League attendance they had played in front of since 63,450 saw the game in the old First Division between the same sides at the same stadium 36 years earlier.

Here's another oddity with which you can poke fun at any of your United-supporting mates.....the three biggest home crowds in United's history are well over 80,000 but, remarkably, were all for games that had to be played at Maine Road, the former HQ of their neighbours Manchester City, following damage to Old Trafford during the Second World War. It was shortly afterwards, in 1949, that Wolves beat United in a semi-final replay on their way to winning the FA Cup but it's not only in Manchester that the Wanderers have proved to be a big draw in their long and proud history.

They are also responsible for the largest-ever turn-out at Anfield, 61,905 having seen them lose an FA Cup fourth-round tie against Liverpool in February, 1952. And they still hold three other attendance records that are unlikely ever to be broken – at Grimsby (31,657 in February, 1937), Blackpool (38,098 in September, 1955) and Coventry (51,455 in April, 1967).

The biggest-ever crowd at Molineux is still the 61,315 who were packed in for the FA Cup fifth-round tie against Liverpool in that triumphant run of 1938-39.

THE ANSWERS...

So how did you fare with our quizzes, anagrams and spot the ball competitions? It's time to check your answers....

Quiz : Know Your Club's Season (from page 46)
1. Stephen Elliott
2. Seyi Olofinjana
3. Stoke City
4. Luton Town
5. England
6. Fifth
7. Andy Keogh
8. George Elokobi
9. Michael Gray
10. Seyi Olofinjana

Anagram Answers (from page 53)
1. Kevin Foley
2. Matt Jarvis
3. Michael Gray
4. George Elokobi
5. David Edwards
6. Michael Kightly
7. Sylvan Ebanks-Blake
8. Sam Vokes
9. Karl Henry
10. Andy Keogh

Quiz : Know Your Club's History (from page 57)
1. Steve Bull
2. John Richards
3. Billy Wright
4. Stan Cullis
5. 1999
6. Stafford Rangers
7. Derek Dougan
8. The Sherpa Van Trophy
9. Graham Turner
10. Graham Taylor

SPOT THE BALL (from page 53)